THE GOVERNMENT AND GEOGRAPHY OF ANCIENT INDIA

GINA HAGLER

ROSEN

Published in 2017 by The Rosen Publishing Group, Inc.
29 East 21st Street, New York, NY 10010

First Edition

Library of Congress Cataloging-in-Publication Data

Names: Hagler, Gina, author.
Title: The government and geography of ancient India / Gina Hagler.
Description: First edition. | New York : Rosen Publishing, 2017. | Series:
 Spotlight on the rise and fall of ancient civilizations | Includes bibliographical
 references and index. | Audience: Grades 7-12.
Identifiers: LCCN 2016000820| ISBN 9781477789360 (library bound) | ISBN
 9781477789346 (pbk.) | ISBN 9781477789353 (6-pack)
Subjects: LCSH: India--Politics and government--To 997. | Geography, Ancient.
 | India--Geography.
Classification: LCC DS451 .H227 2016 | DDC 934--dc23
LC record available at http://lccn.loc.gov/2016000820

Manufactured in the United States of America

CONTENTS

ANCIENT INDIA'S GOVERNMENT AND GEOGRAPHY

India dates back to the time of ancient Egypt and Mesopotamia. Several notable civilizations have ruled over the centuries. The type of government ruling the region has been directly tied to the amount of territory controlled by that civilization.

The Indus Valley Civilization (3000 BCE–1500 BCE) was located on the floodplain of the Indus River. Ruins lead us to believe that there was no one great source of power.

The Mauryan Empire (320–185 BCE) had a very stable centralized government. It also had a standing army for defense. As a result, the Mauryan Empire controlled one of the largest states in ancient times.

The Gupta Empire (320–550 CE) stretched in a band across the top of the Indian subcontinent. The empire was known for cultural and academic excellence, but the government was weak. Civil unrest and invasions from outside led to a small empire.

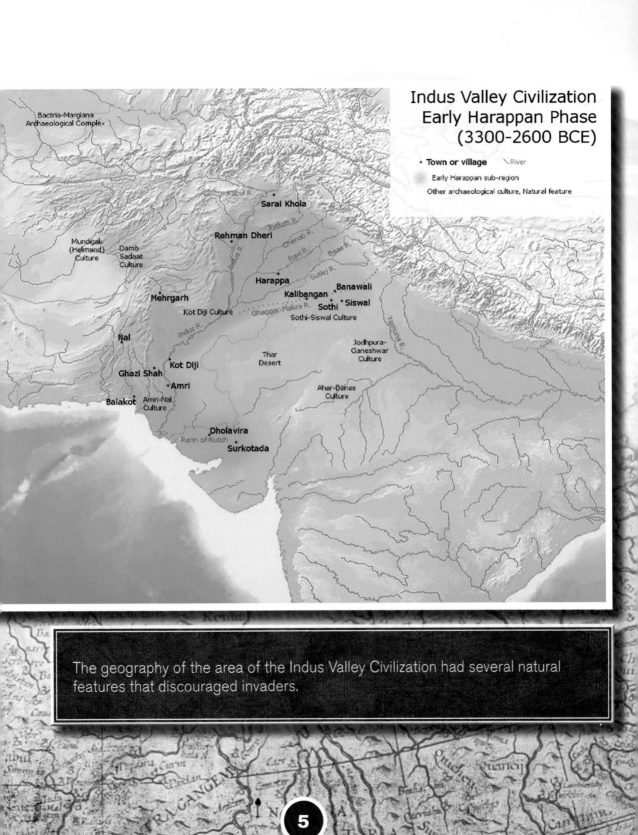

Indus Valley Civilization Early Harappan Phase (3300-2600 BCE)

- Town or village
- River
- Early Harappan sub-region
- Other archaeological culture, Natural feature

Bactria-Margiana Archaeological Complex

Kabul R.

Sarai Khola

Jhelum R.

Rehman Dheri

Chenab R.

Ravi R.

Baas R.

Indus R.

Mundigak (Helmand) Culture

Damb Sadaat Culture

Harappa

Sutlej R.

Banawali

Mehrgarh

Kalibangan

Sothi

Siswal

Kot Diji Culture

Ghaggar-Hakra R.

Sothi-Siswal Culture

Nal

Indus R.

Yamuna R.

Ghazi Shah

Kot Diji

Thar Desert

Jodhpura-Ganeshwar Culture

Amri

Ahar-Banas Culture

Balakot

Amri-Nal Culture

Dholavira

Rann of Kutch

Surkotada

The geography of the area of the Indus Valley Civilization had several natural features that discouraged invaders.

THE CONNECTION BETWEEN GOVERNMENT AND GEOGRAPHY

A government is a group of people or institutions that control and make decisions for a geographic area. A government can share power with its citizens or keep all the power for itself by denying its citizens any form of representation. A government can also be based upon a religious code that makes the responsibilities of its citizens clear.

The geography of a civilization is the amount of territory controlled by that civilization. It may also include some features related to topography such as mountains. To control a large area, a government must be able to enforce its rules and protect its borders. A weak government will not be able to do this. A strong government can, whether it is centralized with the seat of power in one place or decentralized with power spread around the territory and an alliance between those who hold power.

A civilization's territory and the physical features of the land are its geography. Rivers and mountains can be key elements in a civilization's success.

THE INDUS VALLEY CIVILIZATION

The Indus Valley Civilization (3000 BCE–1500 BCE) was a very early civilization that extended from the coast of the Arabian Sea to the Indus floodplain in what is now Pakistan and northwest India. It was at its peak between 2500 and 2000 BCE. Since there are no written records, archaeologists have learned about the civilization from the buildings and artifacts discovered in excavated cities.

There is no evidence of one grand building or city that would have been the center of government. However, there is evidence of a central plan for the large cities that have been unearthed. In these cities, the roads run straight at ninety-degree angles. There are buildings for storing grain, facilities for storing water for irrigation, and evidence of a sanitation system that took wastewater away from the city. All of this required the cooperation of the people and whatever form of government they had.

These ruins are all that is left of the ancient Indus River Valley city of Gujarat. Ruins help us understand early civilizations.

THEOCRACY

Archaeologists theorize that the Indus Valley Civilization was made up of city-states. Each of these city-states was a center of power, but no one power would have been greater than its neighbors. Since each city had a central plan, and all of the cities depended upon the Indus River for water and food, archaeologists theorize that there was some cooperation between these city-states.

Hinduism was beginning to be a part of life in India by the end of the Indus Valley Civilization. Whether it was introduced by the Aryans when they came into power or was already in practice when they arrived is not known. What is theorized is that the governments of the city-states were theocracies. This meant that priests were society's leaders and a deity or god was the supreme civil ruler.

Since a central tenet of Hinduism is the caste system, reinforcement of these beliefs as a way of maintaining a social order was valuable to the Aryans as they came into power.

This carved seal featuring a Brahman bull was found in Mohenjo-Daro. The bull was sacred to Hindus.

KARMA

In a society without a strong centralized government, there must be some way for the people being governed to know what is expected. One way of achieving this is through the social order.

For a theocracy, putting forth a clear social order is not a difficult matter—the belief system is already defined. One advantage of this sort of social order for any theocracy is that there is no need to enforce a large number of civil regulations.

The theology of Hinduism included the concept of Karma. This is the belief that your good deeds will go rewarded just as your bad deeds will be punished.

Since the deeds under consideration were not just the deeds from this life but included deeds from past lives as well, there was little reason for the citizens to be unhappy with the government. Emphasis was placed on personal responsibility. It made ruling a much easier job than it might have been.

This stone carving was found at the Ellora archaeological site in Maharashtra, India. Ellora is a World Heritage Site famous for its monumental caves.

PHYSICAL DESCRIPTION OF THE INDUS VALLEY

The Indus Valley Civilization centered around the Indus River floodplain and delta. Once it was understood that flooding would occur on a regular cycle and that very favorable growing conditions would result, the people who lived in the Indus Valley were able to situate their cities accordingly and ensure themselves of an adequate supply of food for the first time in history.

Along with the river as a source of water and fertile soil, the Indus Valley people had the Himalayan Mountains to the west to serve as a barrier to invaders. They also had mountains to the north, as well as the Arabian Sea to the west. The Thar Desert to the south was just as effective in keeping invaders away. These geographical features discouraged invaders. The Indus River provided a dependable source of water. As a result, the Indus Valley Civilization controlled its territory without the need for an advanced army or strong centralized government.

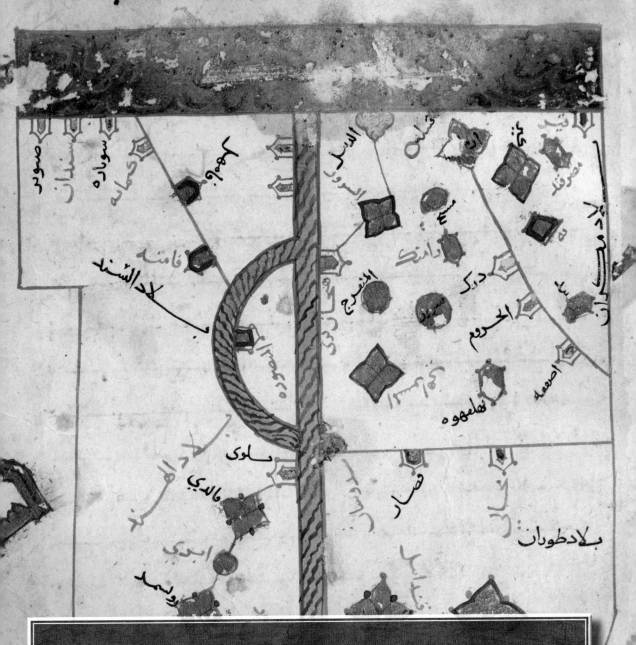

This ancient map shows the Indus River and the civilization that sprung up around it. The physical features of the Indus Valley allowed the civilization to thrive.

INDUS VALLEY CITIES

The major cities of the Indus Valley Civilization were Harappa, Mohenjo-Daro, Mehrgarh, and Lothal. When the walled cities of Harappa and Mohenjo-Daro were excavated, archaeologists were surprised at the level of sophistication. Walls were made of hardened mud bricks. Streets were paved with bricks as well, and they ran straight, at ninety-degree angles. Sanitation systems were in place to carry wastewater away from the water supply and homes of the people. Irrigation systems were in place to ensure ample water for crops and personal use.

Archaeologists also discovered that there was no one city that was grander or greater than another, and there were no great buildings that suggested they housed important functions. This led scholars to believe that material goods were not highly prized and that the cooperation it took to coordinate the plans for the cities was cooperation that existed in other areas of life as well.

Chandragupta Maurya founded the Maurya Empire and unified most of greater India into one state.

DEFENSE AND CURRENCY

The Mauryan Empire had the largest standing army of its time. It included six hundred thousand infantrymen, thirty thousand cavalry, nine thousand war elephants, and eight thousand chariots. It also employed a system of spies to report back on other countries, as well as on its own people. The ability to police and protect its own territory was the result of a strong centralized government.

The Mauryans were active traders throughout the region. They minted their own silver coins in order to facilitate this trade. Large numbers of these coins are still being discovered today, leading scholars to surmise that there were millions of the coins minted.

The majority of the coins have five symbols on one side. The specific symbols and pattern on the coin varies, and today we do not know what the symbols stood for. The large number of coins supports the theory that the Mauryan Empire was very wealthy.

These gold coins depict Mauryan dynasty king Chandragupta and his queen, Durdhara.

TRADE

Trade between countries is a natural way to acquire goods and other materials that are not available in one's own country. A country needs to have a secure base to trade from, since a large amount of goods that are worth something to another group will have to be carried from one location to the next.

If a government is known to be weak, or if there is no army or other way of enforcing their claims on their own goods, trading is not as easy as it seems. Merchants must be confident they can make the trip both ways, with their rights protected, before setting off on a trading expedition.

The Mauryan Empire had a strong government with a large and well-respected professional army. Trading partners knew keeping a good relationship with the Mauryans was good for their interests because the Mauryans would not want any harm to come to the source of the goods they wanted and needed.

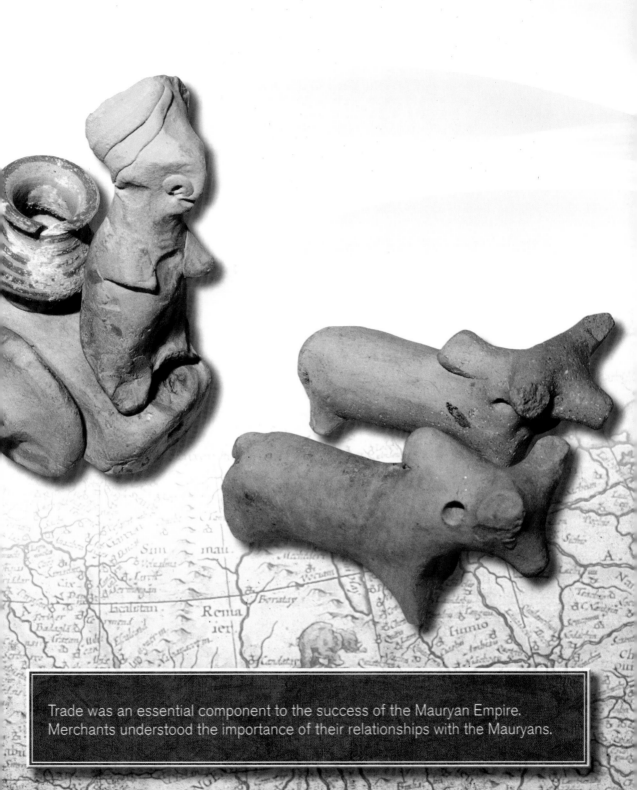

Trade was an essential component to the success of the Mauryan Empire. Merchants understood the importance of their relationships with the Mauryans.

A LARGE GEOGRAPHIC SPAN

The Mauryan Empire was among the largest of its time. It was not easy to rule an area as great as the subcontinent of India during the days before telephone, telegraph, e-mail, fax machines, cars, or airplanes. It required a close attention to detail combined with an efficient and organized system to make sure nothing was overlooked.

The Mauryan kings realized they could not effectively rule such a vast holding from one remote location. They ruled instead by dividing the territory into four provinces. Each province oversaw itself, with all of the provinces reporting to one man who oversaw the provinces, who then reported to other administrators and the king.

To ensure that the empire was free from attack or unrest, the Mauryan kings maintained a large and well-equipped army. This army was made up of professional soldiers. Anyone considering a fight with such an army would have serious reservations.

This is a fragment of a pillar edict of Emperor Ashoka of the Mauryan dynasty. Ashoka was one of the greatest Mauryan leaders.

MAURYAN CITIES

Each of the four provinces of the Mauryan Empire had its own capital city. Taxila was the capital of the northwest province. Ujjain and Suvarnagiri were the capitals of the western and southern provinces, respectively. Pataliputra was the capital of the central province. These capital cities were essential to the centralized government because each of them governed the districts within the city, as well as the villages within the districts.

To carry out the administrative tasks of government, each of the provinces was overseen by a governor. Even though the governors were usually members of the royal family, they were watched by spies who reported back to the king. The districts reported to Sthaniks, the villages to Guptas, and each level of government corresponded to the level of a province, a district, or a village.

In this way, the king could make his home in Pataliputra, yet still be informed of everything going on in his holdings.

This carving of Stupa, an eagle with two heads, was discovered at an archaeological site in Taxila, capital of the northwest province.

THE GUPTA EMPIRE

The Gupta Empire (320–550 CE) is known as a golden era. This is because during this time, art, literature, learning, and trade all flourished. There was peace, ample amounts of food, and freedom from widespread death caused by battle or illness.

Artisans worked in specialized areas to produce goods, and production levels were high enough to provide materials for trade. The Guptas controlled a smaller territory than the Mauryans, but the prosperity and intellectual blossoming of the time were unprecedented.

When Chandragupta came to power, all he had was control of several rich veins of iron. He added to his power by marrying a princess from an adjacent kingdom. This allowed him to control trade on the Ganges River.

Once he took possession of the land to the west, ending at the Arabian Sea, he had access to both the Ganges and travel by sea.

The Gupta Empire was the golden age for the arts, among other things.

GUPTA LEADERS

Sri Gupta (reigned 240–280 CE) established the Gupta Empire. His grandson Chandragupta I (r. 320–335 CE), expanded the empire and was considered by many to be the King of Kings, or Maharajadhiraj. Samudragupta (r. 332–375 CE) achieved peace in the lands conquered by Chandragupta by making his enemies kings in what had been their seats of power before conquest. The empire grew in size and prestige, becoming very wealthy in the process. Samudragupta issued gold coins.

Chandragupta II (r. 375–415 CE) was one of the most powerful rulers of the Gupta Empire and ruled during the period known as the Golden Age. Kumaragupta I (r. 415–455 CE) was Chandragupta II's son. He fought to maintain the territory in the Gupta Empire. Skandagupta was the last of the great Gupta rulers. The Gupta Empire was under frequent attack during his reign. He defeated the White Huns, but ultimately the empire went into decline and ended in 550 CE.

Chandragupta I should not be confused with Chandragupta Maurya, pictured above.

A WEAK GOVERNMENT

During the time of Chandragupta I and Samudragupta, the Gupta government was strong and the empire was wealthy and successful. A number of factors, internal and external, led to the failure of the government and its resulting inability to maintain the empire.

One problem was that the Gupta Empire was coming under repeated attack from outside. Each of the invasion attempts had to be fought off. This took a tremendous amount of resources.

Another problem was that there was often disagreement within the royal family, as well as unrest in the provinces. Many of the territories that had been conquered wanted their independence.

This unrest required attention and led to bad feelings and a lack of cooperation. All in all, the tremendous pressure on the king and the economic pressure on the empire in its last years ultimately led to the end of the Gupta Empire.

This Gupta carving depicts two warriors with a griffon. Gupta warriors found themselves defending the empire almost constantly.

THE CASTE SYSTEM

One aspect of the Gupta Empire that may have helped its rulers during its decline is the existence of the caste system. The Gupta Empire was not a theocracy, so religious leaders were not the rulers, but the caste system did provide a strict social structure.

Under the caste system, people and their descendants were born into a class that would be theirs for life. Only after death and rebirth might someone's soul advance within the system. The system allowed for Brahmins (priests), Kshatriyas (warriors), Vaishyas (merchants and landowners), Shudras (servants and subordinates), and Untouchables (the lowest of the low).

The caste system would be outlawed in 1950 CE, but, especially in ancient times, it was a very efficient way of limiting the extent of civil unrest; the people might want independence from the empire, but they did not seek a complete overthrow of the social order.

The caste system confined citizens to a strict social structure. At the bottom of the hierarchy were the Untouchables. This photograph was taken in the 1930s, not long before the end of the caste system.

THE EXTENT OF THE GUPTA EMPIRE

Given the growing threat of invasion and the extent of unrest within the conquered territories, the extent of the Gupta Empire fluctuated. Part of this was because of pressure from the evolving civilizations to the north and west. Part of this was the wish of conquered people to regain their freedom, most probably a result of having been given some authority over themselves during the time of Samudragupta.

A great deal of resources went to fund the arts and other endeavors that created the Golden Age. This took money out of the economy, while making the area attractive to those seeking to have it as their own.

Ultimately, the balance of power and geography for the Gupta Empire resulted in control of northern India from the Gangetic Plain in the east to the Arabian Sea to the west. At various times during the empire, greater areas to the south were included.

This carving of Vishnu was found in the Udayagiri Caves, an early Hindu ritual site in the state of Madhya Pradesh in northern India. The caves are one of India's most important archaeological sites from the Gupta period.

INDIA TODAY

Today India is the largest country in South Asia. Twenty-nine states and seven union territories comprise this federal republic with a population second only to China. New Delhi is the capital, and India has fourteen official languages, with Hindi the most prominent. While not one of the official languages, English is the most important language for the central government, official communications, and the commercial sector.

India is the world's largest democracy and provides living proof that people from a wide range of backgrounds and religious beliefs can work and live together successfully. The stable centralized government of today provides a voice for the people with a bureaucracy to oversee the day-to-day operation of the government and provide needed services.

The stable political system forms a background for rapid growth in the business sectors as India strives to take its place in the world economy.

Today, Raisina Hill in New Delhi is home to Rashtrapati Bhavan, the official residence of the president of India, as well as several other important offices and government ministries.

GLOSSARY

Buddhism A set of spiritual beliefs based upon the teachings of Gautama Buddha.

caste system The rigid social hierarchy that is part of Hinduism.

centralized Power held by a small group or in one location.

civil Within a group, country, or civilization.

civilization An advanced state of society where a new level of culture or science has been achieved.

decline A gradual loss of strength or power.

dynasty A series of rulers from one family.

election The process through which citizens choose leaders by voting.

empire Vast land holdings made up of states or countries under a single authority.

flourish To grow in healthy and vigorous ways, often because of favorable economic or environmental reasons.

invasion An attack by parties from outside of a group, country, or civilization.

natural defense Protection afforded by geographic features such as mountains, deserts, or bodies of water.

province An administrative area within a country.

representation Having one's wishes carried out by another.

republic Government where power is held by elected representatives.

social order The ways that a government and society are expected to behave.

stable Unvarying, constant; not prone to large fluctuations.

subcontinent A subdivision of a continent that is of significant size and largely self-contained.

theocracy Government where priests or other clergy are leaders and a deity or god is the supreme civil ruler.

unrest Unhappiness and action taken in reaction to the current social order.

FOR MORE INFORMATION

Asia Society and Museum
725 Park Avenue (at 70th Street)
New York, NY 20021
(212) 288-6400
Web site: http://asiasociety.org/india-historical-overview
The Asia Society is an educational organization that promotes Asian
art, culture, business, and policy. There are offices in Hong Kong,
Houston, Los Angeles, Manila, Melbourne, Mumbai, New York, San
Francisco, Seoul, Shanghai, Washington, D.C., and Zurich.

Grameen Foundation
1101 15th Street NW
3rd Floor
Washington, DC 20005
(202) 628-3560
Web site: http://www.grameenfoundation.org/where-we-work/asia/india
The Grameen Foundation provides financial and technical support to
microfinance and social enterprises in India. It also works to bring
mobile health initiatives to the people of India through its MO-
TECH Platform.

The Indian Archaeological Society
B-17, Qutab Institutional Area,
New Delhi 110016
India
Web site: http://ichr.ac.in
The Indian Archaeological Society was formed and registered in 1967.
Its purpose is to encourage archaeological study of ancient India,
as well as sharie the findings.

Indian Council of Historical Research
35 Ferozeshah Road
New Delhi 110 001
India
Web site: http://ichr.ac.in
The Indian Council of Historical Research was founded in 1972 for
    the purpose of bringing historians together to conduct and share
    research on the history of India.

Society of Ancient Military Historians
Department of History
Western Illinois University
Morgan Hall 445
Macomb, IL 61455-1390
(309) 298-1053
Web site: http://ccat.sas.upenn.edu/rrice/samh.html
The Society of Ancient Military Historians (SAMH) is dedicated to the
    study of warfare in the ancien world. It promotes contact between
    members and within the larger academic community.

WEBSITES

Because of the changing nature of Internet links, Rosen Publishing has
developed an online list of websites related to the subject of this book.
This site is updated regularly. Please use this link to access the list:

http://www.rosenlinks.com/SRFAC/igov

FOR FURTHER READING

Avari, Burjor. *India: The Ancient Past: A History of the Indian Subcontinent from C. 7000 BCE to 1200 CE*. New York, NY: Routledge, 2016.

Basu, Soma. *Warfare in Ancient India: In Historical Outline*. New Delhi, India: D.K. Printworld, 2014.

Eck, Diana L. *India: A Sacred Geography*. New York, NY: Harmony Books, 2012.

Holm, Kirsten C. *Everyday Life in Ancient India*. New York, NY: PowerKids Press, 2012.

Kapur, Akash. *India Becoming: A Portrait of Life in Modern India*. New York, NY: Riverhead Books, 2012.

Keay, John. *India a History: From the Earliest Civilisations to the Boom of the Twenty-First Century*. London, England: HarperCollins, 2013.

Lassieur, Allison. *Ancient India*. New York, NY: Children's Press, 2013.

Norwich, John J. *Cities That Shaped the Ancient World*. New York, NY: Thames & Hudson, 2014.

Roxburgh, Ellis. *The Mauryan Empire of India*. New York, NY: Cavendish Square Publishing, 2016.

Turner, Tracey, and Jamie Lenman. *Hard as Nails Kings and Queens*. New York, NY: Crabtree Publishing Company, 2016.

Williams, Marcia. *The Elephant's Friend and Other Tales from Ancient India*. Somerville, MA: Candlewick Press, 2014.

BIBLIOGRAPHY

Aronovsky, Ilona, and Sujata Gopinath. *The Indus Valley*. Oxford, England: Heinemann Library, 2005.

Avari, Burjor. *India: The Ancient Past: A History of the Indian Subcontinent from C. 7000 BCE to 1200 CE*. New York, NY: Routledge, 2016.

Bowden, Rob. *Settlements of the Indus River*. Oxford, England: Heinemann Library, 2005.

"Civilization: The Mauryan Empire of Ancient India." TimeMaps Ltd, 2015. Retrieved December 10, 2015 (http://www.timemaps.com/civilization-the-mauryan-empire).

"Gupta Empire Leaders." TheIndianHistory.org. Retrieved December 10, 2015 (http://www.theindianhistory.org/Gupta/gupta-empire-leaders.html).

"Indus Valley: Technology and Jobs." BBC, 2014. Retrieved December 10, 2015 (http://www.bbc.co.uk/schools/primaryhistory/indus_valley/technology_and_jobs).

Kautilya, and L. N. Rangarajan, ed. *The Arthashastra*. New Delhi, India: Penguin Books India, 1992.

Machiavelli, Niccolò, and George Bull, trans. *The Prince*. London, England: Penguin Books, 1999.

Robinson, Francis. *The Cambridge Encyclopedia of India, Pakistan, Bangladesh, Sri Lanka, Nepal, Bhutan, and the Maldives*. Cambridge, England: Cambridge University Press, 1989.

The Story of India." PBS. MayaVision International, 2008. Retrieved December 10, 2015 (http://www.pbs.org/thestoryofindia).

Sunzi, and Samuel B. Griffith, trans. *The Art of War*. London, England: Oxford University Press, 1971.

"The World Factbook–India." Central Intelligence Agency. Retrieved December 10, 2015 (https://www.cia.gov/library/publications/the-world-factbook/geos/in.html).

INDEX

ABOUT THE AUTHOR

Gina Hagler writes about history and social studies. She has a lifelong interest in politics and the history of warfare, as well as the ways in which technological advances influence the outcome of conflict. She is the author of many history, science, and technology books for young adults and young readers. You can see these titles at her author page, amazon.com/author/ginahagler, and read more about history, science, and technology on her blog, http://www.ginahagler.com.

PHOTO CREDITS